#SCARS

SURVIVORS CARRY A REAL STORY

Your voice.
Your story.
It matters.

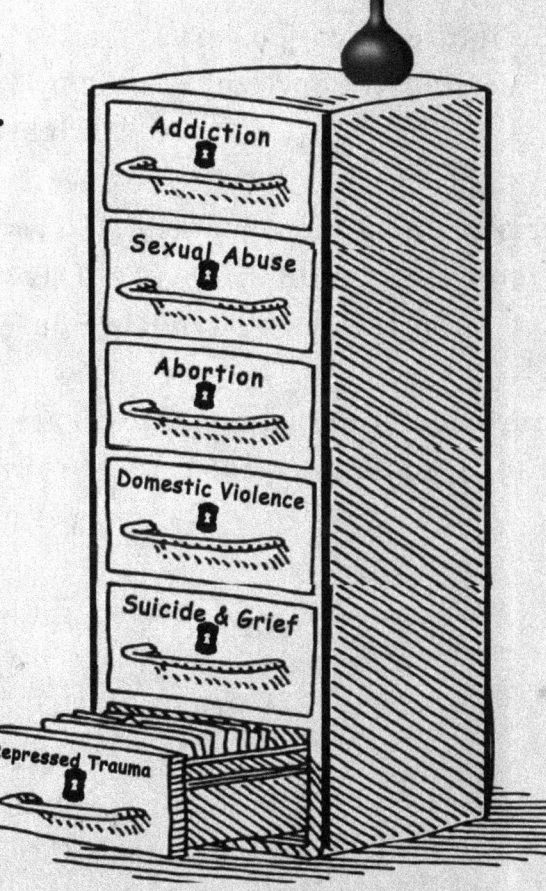

KRISTEN KELLETT

Copyright © 2023 A Door of Hope International
SCARS of Sexual Abuse Student Manual
ISBN: 979-8-9877230-6-7

No part of this book may be used or reproduced by any means, graphic, electronic, or mechanical, including photocopying, recording, taping, or by any information storage retrieval system without the written permission of the publisher except in the case of brief quotations.

Scripture quotations marked (NLT) are taken from the New Living Translation, copyright © 1996, 2004, 2015 by Tyndale House Foundation. Used by permission of Tyndale House Publishers, Carol Stream, Illinois 60188. All rights reserved. Scripture quotations marked (NKJV) are taken from the New King James Version®. Copyright © 1982 by Thomas Nelson. Used by permission. All rights reserved.

Scripture quotations marked MSG are taken from THE MESSAGE, copyright © 1993, 2002, 2018 by Eugene H. Peterson. Used by permission of NavPress, represented by Tyndale House Publishers. All rights reserved.

Scripture quotations marked (AMP) are taken from the Amplified Bible, Copyright © 1954, 1958, 1962, 1964, 1965, 1987 by The Lockman Foundation. Used by permission.

Printed in the United States

A DOOR OF HOPE INTERNATIONAL
Kristen Kellett
PO Box 37095
Panama City, Florida 32412
kristen@adoorofhopeinternational.com

I began my journey of healing as a client of A Door of Hope in 2015. I had been sexually abused by my stepfather for 8 years. I knew God was wanting me to deal with the childhood sexual abuse that seemed to dominate my every action and thought. I just couldn't get over the trauma that I experienced. The staff at A Door of Hope was loving, kind and compassionate to me as we walked together, exchanging the lies that I believed about myself and the abuse that happened to me with the truth of God's Word and who He says I am. The training has helped me to finally walk in freedom and begin to accept God's love for me. It has helped to prepare me to actively be in ministry and give back to others.

Glory Riggins
Trauma Survivor

Kristen is very knowledgeable when it comes to the healing of life-controlling issues and self-destructive behaviors. She has a unique way of explaining the dynamics of trauma, so that the root cause can be found. As a trauma coach and a survivor of many different traumas myself, Kristen has walked me through my own healing process of multiple past abortions. These were hidden traumas that needed to be uprooted. I was not able to fully walk into the purpose that God had on my life until I went back to heal the wounds of my past. Kristen's trainings played a pivotal roll in my healing process. Understanding how trauma affects the brain and the body is essential for healing. These trainings will not only change your life, they will change your perspective about life. You'll even have a greater understanding of your loved ones, and the people that you come in contact with daily. I highly recommend these trauma trainings.

Shona Chavis
Trauma coach
a voice Awakening

I was a survivor of childhood sexual abuse [CSA] from the ages of 2-16 years old. In my adult years, looking back, I can see all the damage that took place was the result of my upbringing. There was self-doubt, insecurities, self-harm and wrong relationships, just to mention a few. For years, I sought counseling, doctors, and help with the many issues that come from CSA, but to no avail. When I met Kristen Kellett, she was launching A Door of Hope. I knew at that moment I wanted to be a part of what she was building. One of the requirements for working with A Door of Hope was we first had to go through these Trauma Trainings to be able to work with women coming out of trauma. Little did I know that I needed the training to work through issues I assumed were long dealt with. After several counseling sessions and lots of tears, I was finally free from the trauma of CSA. This training is much needed for every person who has experienced CSA. The trainings that A Door of Hope International brings deal with many issues, not just CSA, but in a way that the person can receive. These trauma trainings are God-breathed. In 2014, there was a fire birthed within me to help others who have suffered CSA. Now with the training I have received, I counsel with girls and women where they are, and it brings me much joy to tell them, "I understand, and here's why," then I am able to share the freedom and joy that they can have because there is truly hope after trauma.

Kathryn Hoyt
"SOAR"
Survivor Of Abuse Rising up

Survivors of traumatic events often feel trapped—unable to carry on with normal life because their emotional pain keeps them locked in the past. SCARS Trauma Training gives a biblical foundation along with the personal testimony of one survivor to another, proving that God's ability to heal is stronger than trauma's ability to wound. The training will help you identify trauma and gives guidelines for intervention and counseling tools.

Cindy Brengosz
Executive Director
First Choice Pregnancy Resource Center

As a pastor and in ministry with Kristen Kellett for many years, I highly recommend SCARS Training Manuals of A Door of Hope International. I have worked alongside Kristen in A Door of Hope Ministries and the staff and volunteers were trained through this material. This training prepares you, your staff, and your church to empower women in crisis.

We as a Church need to help hurting people, and most of us pastors have never been exposed to most traumas as addiction, childhood sexual abuse, domestic violence, and suicide, but this Training Manual can prepare you and push you forward to deep healings inside your church body. I encourage each of you to invite Kristen Kellett to train you and your staff to be ready for the next level.

Running for His Purpose,
Pastor Louise Cook
Streams of Refreshing Church
Walker, Louisiana

SCARS

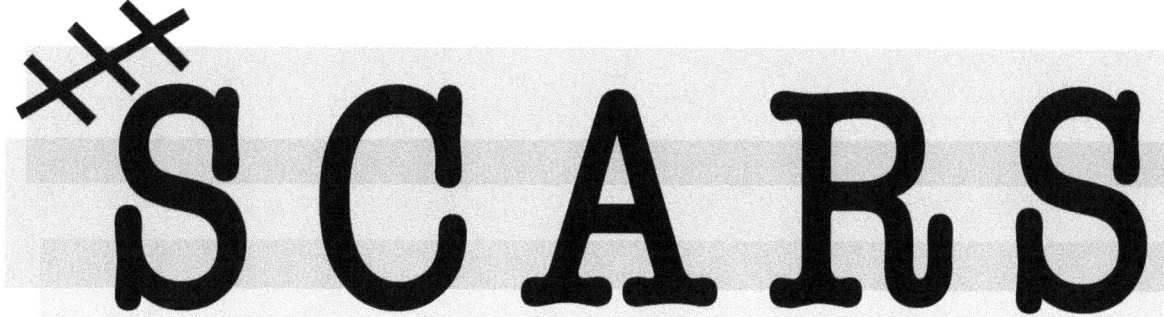

SCARS

SURVIVORS CARRY A REAL STORY
OF SEXUAL ABUSE

STUDENT MANUAL

Kristen Kellett
FOREWORD BY JANE HAMON

A Door of Hope International

MISSION

A Door of Hope International is a non-profit organization whose mission is to support, promote, and enhance the spiritual lives of women. Our purpose is to break the cycle of life-controlling issues and self-destructive behaviors rooted in trauma through the transforming love and power of Jesus Christ to restore hope, healing, and freedom with the intention of connecting trauma survivors to their God-given purpose.

VISION

A Door of Hope International is a faith based, non-profit organization whose primary focus is to equip individuals, churches, and organizations, including but not limited to domestic violence shelters, pregnancy resource centers, addiction treatment and support, those working with victims of human trafficking, prison ministries, half-way houses, homeless shelters, churches and those who work with female trauma survivors by providing training in trauma, resources, and support.

Foreword

We live in a fallen world. It's hard to fathom the pain and cruelty one human can inflict on another out of his or her own dysfunction or dark soul. It's hard to process the loss of a parent or loved one due to an accident, sickness, drugs, alcohol or some other irresponsible behavior. It's heartbreaking to deal with the trauma an individual experiences due to war, weather or other catastrophic events. It's especially difficult to live a healed, whole, happy life if a person experienced these wounds as a child.

But there is hope. God looked down on this fallen world and sent a Savior, Jesus Christ. He didn't just come to save our eternal souls from hell, but also came to bring hope to the hopeless and healing to those living in despair. Jesus, himself, suffered the trauma of the cross at his death. However, throughout his life he was faced with all of life's challenges. His birth occurred in a way that many believed him to be illegitimate during an era where this brought great shame. He was born during a time of incredible poverty as the country he was born into was ruled by a cruel, unjust army. His birth triggered the slaughter of all male babies under the age of two, which caused he and his family to flee to a foreign land. In ministry he was misunderstood by his family, rejected by those he came to help, forsaken by his friends, publicly humiliated, falsely accused and physically abused leading to a criminal's death. He did all this so he could carry our pain, our grief, our sorrow and through his wounds ours are healed.

I have been in ministry for over forty years and have counseled many people who have been broken through life's traumas yet have seen them get healed of their pain and grief and go on to live happy, whole lives. I was a victim of childhood sexual abuse, so I understand the pain some live with their entire lives, along with the physical, emotional, and mental impact of their trauma. But no matter the pain or the shame of what an individual has walked through, there is hope, help and freedom through Christ. At times healing comes supernaturally through a personal encounter with the Lord. More often it comes through sharing and receiving counsel from someone trained to facilitate healing.

This is why I applaud Kristen Kellett for pouring her heart and years of expertise into this powerful tool of hope and healing. She has spent years seeing lives transformed by biblical principles and God's anointing and grace. Scars will empower individuals to become ambassadors of hope and freedom to those who have been bound in pain. Rise to the challenge to become a freedom maker!

Jane Hamon

Apostle, Vision Church @ Christian International

Author: *Dreams & Visions, Discernment, Declarations for Breakthrough* and *The Deborah Company*

Contents

Foreword	i
Introduction	v
01 Sexual Abuse Awareness	**1**
What is childhood sexual abuse?	1
Characteristics of a Child Abuser	2
Repressed vs Suppressed Memories	3
Triggers	3
Flashbacks	4
Trigger Toolkit	5
Stitching Them Back Up	8
02 Effects on Survivors	**9**
Effects of Sexual Trauma	11
Identifying Behavior Patterns in Survivors	12
Three Personality Profiles Often Seen in Survivors	18
03 Survival Skills	**21**
Helping Survivors Move Forward	23
What Do You Believe?	24
Forgiveness vs. Unforgiveness	27

04 Working With Survivors ... 31
    Characteristics of an Effective Peer Supporter ... 31
    Reasons we refer a client to another person. ... 33
    Activation ... 34
    Self-Care Assessment ... 35

Resources ... 39

Exit Survey ... 41

Endnotes ... 43

Introduction

I have spent over twenty years working with female survivors. I cannot convey how much respect I have for these women, not only for having the courage to break their silence, but also for having the boldness to face their fears and share their stories.

I have worked with women in their sixties and seventies who carried their secret for decades, never sharing the traumatic experiences of what happened when they were little girls. They have invited me into their pain, into the very places they have kept private until they were ready to share. By providing a safe space of support, they have been able to unlock the places that have held them back so that God could bring healing to those areas. By finding their voice, they have been able to release their pain and move forward.

After seeing the need to train others in providing trauma informed care, we have shifted our focus to provide training to both men and women.

I am not a licensed professional. I do not have a college degree. Although I am certified in trauma recovery and have training in various areas of trauma, I am not a licensed counselor. I am, however, passionate about helping survivors get from feeling stuck or barely surviving to a place where they are thriving. Nothing satisfies me more than empowering others to fulfill their destiny. There is a reason you survived. You survived for a purpose.

This training manual contains years of personal experience, biblical examples, and practical tools that will help you in working with survivors of trauma.

THE PURPOSE OF THIS SCARS TRAINING IS TO BRING AWARENESS CONCERNING THE EFFECTS OF TRAUMA AS RELATED TO SEXUAL ABUSE AND PROVIDE INSIGHT INTO HOW UNTREATED TRAUMA AFFECTS US IN ADULTHOOD. THIS TRAINING WILL EQUIP YOU WITH TOOLS FOR CRISIS INTERVENTION WHEN WORKING WITH FEMALE SURVIVORS. INCLUDED IS A LIST OF NATIONAL HOTLINE NUMBERS THAT CAN PROVIDE DIRECT ASSISTANCE.

DISCLOSURE: Please be advised that SCARS depicts experiences as related to trauma. In today's training, participants who have been victims themselves may find parts of this training triggering—in terms of both memories and strong emotions. If this occurs, participants are encouraged to write down their triggers. The participant may choose to take a break or stop participation in the training altogether. If these symptoms occur or persist, seek help with a professional who specializes in trauma.

FOR YOUR SAFETY: If you need to leave the room for any reason, please give us a thumbs up to let our team know you are okay. Otherwise, we will send someone to check on you to see if you need support.

SCARS STANDS FOR SURVIVORS CARRY A REAL STORY

01

Sexual Abuse Awareness

WHAT IS CHILDHOOD SEXUAL ABUSE?

Child sexual abuse can include sexual contact with a child, but it may also include other actions, like exposing oneself, sharing obscene images, or taking inappropriate photos or videos of a child. These crimes can have a serious impact on the life and development of a child, and often continue to impact them later in life.

STATISTICS

It is estimated that,
- Every 68 seconds in the United States, a victim is sexually assaulted. And every nine minutes, that victim is a child.[1]
- 1 in 5 children are solicited for sex on the internet.[2]
- *1 in 4 girls* and nearly *1 in 6 boys* are sexually abused before the age of 18.
- 46% of imprisoned sex offenders who show a persistent pattern of sexually abusing children were, themselves, sexually abused as children.[3]

Children are taught to avoid strangers, often with the common phrase "stranger danger" as a reminder. But strangers are the least common offender:

CHARACTERISTICS OF A CHILD ABUSER

An abuser may exhibit the following behaviors:

All sexual abuse is traumatic. It can have significant negative, reoccurring impact on a person's life if suppressed and left untreated.

Even if it only happened one time.
- One time is all it takes to rob a child's innocence and create long-term effects.
- Sometimes, survivors don't share about the one time it happened because they compare their experience with other survivors who endured prolonged abuse and feel that their one time is insignificant.

If it keeps coming up,
if it is causing you pain,
it's significant.

Pain itself isn't the problem. It lets us know something is wrong and needs our attention, to be treated and dealt with.

Carrying Trauma

Our soul is like a filing cabinet containing files, where both good and bad memories are stored. Sometimes, we have kept these memories repressed or suppressed, filed away, locked and secured, kept confidential, until something or someone triggers us, causing those memories to resurface.

REPRESSED VS SUPPRESSED MEMORIES

Repression is when something traumatic happens that causes the victim to have no memory or recollection of the event.

Suppression is a conscience effort to subdue painful memories.

When triggers and flashbacks happen, the memory is brought to the surface. A survivor who has successfully avoided feeling emotions connected to the trauma suddenly experiences a flood of emotions that need to be processed.

TRIGGERS

A trigger is something that evokes a memory of past traumatizing events, including the feelings and sensations associated with those experiences.

A trigger is a reminder of a past trauma. This reminder can cause a person to feel overwhelming sadness, anxiety, or panic.

VARIOUS TYPES OF TRIGGERS:
- Sight.
- Sound.
- Smell.
- Touch.

EXAMPLES OF TRIGGERS:
- MUSIC:
- SMELLS:
- TASTE, TOUCH, TEXTURE:
- A PLACE:
- A NOISE:
- A WORD:
- A TIME:
- A PERSON:
- NAMES:

FLASHBACKS

A flashback is a sudden and disturbing vivid memory of an event in the past, typically as the result of psychological trauma. A flashback can cause the following:

- Heart begins to beat faster.
- May feel physically sick.
- Mind begins to race.
- Shortness of breath.
- A panic attack.

EXAMPLES OF FLASHBACKS:

Someone shared *wearing a mask* (during the Covid pandemic) *was a trigger* for them.

STEPS FOR MANAGING FLASHBACKS

1. Recognize that you are having a flashback, a present feeling of a past incident.
2. Remind yourself these feelings of my past cannot hurt me now.
3. Establish boundaries that feel safe. For example, if the flashback happens when you see your uncle who abused you at your parents' house, it's okay to decide, "I will only go to my parents' house when my uncle is not there."
4. Be patient with yourself. This is part of healing the little girl inside you who was hurt. Remind yourself that you are no longer in danger. You are safe now.
5. Find someone you trust who can support you as you heal.

DISTINGUISHING A REAL FLASHBACK

What do you do if you're not sure a memory is real? For example, the sexual abuse that happened when I was six surfaced in a dream. At first, I wasn't sure it was real. Here is a determining factor: *if it is causing you pain, then you need to deal with it.*

DENIAL

Denial happens when we ignore symptoms and emotions associated with trauma by using other methods to bury it. Denial is not dealing with what we are truly feeling. It can also be like the ostrich that sticks its head in the sand to avoid danger.

DEFLECTING

We train ourselves to wear a mask or cover our pain with makeup, so no one will see our scars. We could be bleeding internally, but we tell everyone, "I'm doing good! How are you?" This is called deflecting.

We turn the focus off of ourselves and in a different direction in an effort to avoid dealing with our own trauma. We try to fix everyone else's pain when we ourselves are hemorrhaging.

When the shock wears off:
- You're bleeding. (I am?)
- Did you know that you have had a bad attitude? (I do?)
- Do you realize you have been emotionally unavailable? (I have?)

It's okay to not be okay. Healing is a process. Sometimes, it's not a quick fix. The good news is there is progress in the process.

> "GIVE YOURSELF PERMISSION TO DEAL AND HEAL, OR YOU'LL CONTINUE TO BE STUCK ON A TREADMILL."
> - KRISTEN KELLETT

When a survivor is describing details of her experiences, she often feels as though she is reliving the trauma. Her nervous system may become activated. She may experience symptoms related to trauma, such as crying, shortness of breath, strong emotion, etc. and need help returning to the present. Here are some techniques that can be helpful. This is a handout that you can provide to survivors you work with.

Trigger Toolkit

There will be times during your journey of trauma recovery when you may experience triggers, flashbacks of memories and strong emotions. We have included a trigger toolkit with tools that will help you regulate your nervous system should this occur

Developing a trigger toolkit now ensures that when we are triggered, we only have to pull out our fully stocked toolkit and select the coping strategy that best fits the situation.

The below trigger toolkit contains five categories of coping strategies: grounding, resolving, affirming, distracting, and self-soothing.[4]

1. GROUNDING

These interrupt the overwhelming feelings and thoughts swirling around inside our heads by shifting our attention to our bodies, which helps us feel calmer, more focused and more in control of ourselves.

EXAMPLES OF GROUNDING:

2. RESOLVING

These address the underlying cause of particular triggers so that they are no longer a source of being triggered in the future.

EXAMPLES OF RESOLVING:

3. AFFIRMING

These directly impact the way we talk to and think about ourselves and our triggers, making it easier for us to feel in control of our triggers rather than being at their mercy.

EXAMPLES OF AFFIRMING:

4. DISTRACTING

These strategies do not resolve or change our response to a trigger. Instead, they shift our focus from the emotional and physical response to the trigger onto a calmer, emotionally neutral situation, or event. This effectively starves our trigger response, and it dissipates without our attention.

EXAMPLES OF DISTRACTING:

5. SELF-SOOTHING

These are strategies we can implement to soothe and calm the distress caused by a trigger.

EXAMPLES OF SELF-SOOTHING:

These are only a small sampling of the possible coping tools you can develop and keep handy in your trigger toolkit. Experiment with what works for you. Get rid of tools that don't work and hone those that do. Be alert for ideas and suggestions for other tools, so you can continually update and add to your list of coping strategies. In time, you will assemble a highly effective toolkit that provides you with everything you need to both eliminate and cope with any triggers that you may encounter.

> ♡♡
> YOUR TRAUMA IS VALID EVEN IF YOU NEVER TOLD ANYONE, YOU CAN'T REMEMBER ALL OF IT, IT HAPPENED A LONG TIME AGO, PEOPLE DIDN'T BELIEVE YOU, YOU DIDN'T REALIZE IT WAS TRAUMATIC UNTIL LATER, YOU KNOW PEOPLE WHO HAVE BEEN THROUGH "WORSE," YOUR LIFE WASN'T THREATENED, IT DIDN'T DEVELOP INTO PTSD, OR YOU ARE FEELING BETTER NOW.

Stitching Them Back Up

When a survivor has relived her trauma, poured out her heart, it is like open heart surgery (not physically, but spiritually and emotionally). You cannot close a session if she is still activated. It is important to "stitch" her back up. Before the end of your session with her, affirm her, validate her feelings, speak a word of knowledge, and if she will allow, pray into the situation with her/for her. These are ways of stitching her back up, closing the open wound. She may have a scar, but remember, a scar implies that a wound has healed. Her scars are her testimony.

02

Effects on Survivors

BIBLICAL EXAMPLE: TAMAR'S FILE

If we were to look at the counseling notes written in Tamar's file, what would we find, looking at her story through the eyes of trauma? Let's look at 2 Samuel 13:

> Now David's son Absalom had a beautiful sister named Tamar. And Amnon, her half brother, fell desperately in love with her. Amnon became so obsessed with Tamar that he became ill. She was a virgin, and Amnon thought he could never have her.
>
> But Amnon had a very crafty friend—his cousin Jonadab. He was the son of David's brother Shimea. One day Jonadab said to Amnon, "What's the trouble? Why should the son of a king look so dejected morning after morning?"
>
> So Amnon told him, "I am in love with Tamar, my brother Absalom's sister."
>
> "Well," Jonadab said, "I'll tell you what to do. Go back to bed and pretend you are ill. When your father comes to see you, ask him to let Tamar come and prepare some food for you. Tell him you'll feel better if she prepares it as you watch and feeds you with her own hands."
>
> So Amnon lay down and pretended to be sick. And when the king came to see him, Amnon asked him, "Please let my sister Tamar come and cook my favorite dish as I watch. Then I can eat it from her own hands." So David agreed

and sent Tamar to Amnon's house to prepare some food for him.

When Tamar arrived at Amnon's house, she went to the place where he was lying down so he could watch her mix some dough. Then she baked his favorite dish for him. But when she set the serving tray before him, he refused to eat. "Everyone get out of here," Amnon told his servants. So they all left. Then he said to Tamar, "Now bring the food into my bedroom and feed it to me here." So Tamar took his favorite dish to him. But as she was feeding him, he grabbed her and demanded, "Come to bed with me, my darling sister." "No, my brother!" she cried. "Don't be foolish! Don't do this to me! Such wicked things aren't done in Israel. Where could I go in my shame? And you would be called one of the greatest fools in Israel. Please, just speak to the king about it, and he will let you marry me."

But Amnon wouldn't listen to her, and since he was stronger than she was, he raped her. Then suddenly Amnon's love turned to hate, and he hated her even more than he had loved her. "Get out of here!" he snarled at her.

"No, no!" Tamar cried. "Sending me away now is worse than what you've already done to me."

But Amnon wouldn't listen to her. He shouted for his servant and demanded, "Throw this woman out, and lock the door behind her!"

So the servant put her out and locked the door behind her. She was wearing a long, beautiful robe, as was the custom in those days for the king's virgin daughters. But now Tamar tore her robe and put ashes on her head. And then, with her face in her hands, she went away crying.

Her brother Absalom said to her, "Has your brother Amnon had his way with you? Now, my dear sister, let's keep it quiet—a family matter. He is, after all, your brother. Don't take this so hard." Tamar lived in her brother Absalom's home, bitter and desolate.

King David heard the whole story and was enraged, but he didn't discipline Amnon. David doted on him because he was his firstborn. Absalom quit speaking to Amnon—not a word, whether good or bad—because he hated him for violating his sister Tamar. (MSG)

Example: "I walked in without giving it a second thought. Alarms should have sounded in my head, screaming at me, not to go in some stranger's apartment. I didn't know that part of my brain wasn't working."[5]

Effects of Sexual Trauma

The following statistics are estimates:
- 94% of women who are raped experience symptoms of post-traumatic stress disorder (PTSD) during the two weeks following the rape.
- 30% of women report symptoms of PTSD nine months after the rape.
- 33% of women who are raped contemplate suicide.
- 13% of women who are raped attempt suicide.
- Approximately 70% of rape or sexual assault victims experience moderate to severe distress, a larger percentage than for any other violent crime.[6]

POST TRAUMATIC STRESS DISORDER (PTSD):
PTSD is an anxiety disorder brought on by acute trauma that is characterized by recurring thoughts, dreams, distress, triggers, or flashbacks that affect one's ability to cope with everyday life.[7]

CPTSD: COMPLEX POST TRAUMATIC STRESS DISORDER:
CPTSD is a condition that results from chronic or long-term exposure to emotional, physical,

or sexual trauma, over which a victim has little or no control and from which there is little or no hope of escape.[8]

Identifying Behavior Patterns in Survivors

BEHAVIOR #1: DETACHMENT

HEALTHY ATTACHMENT CYCLE

- Baby has a need (wet/hungry); expresses a need (fusses, cries).
- Mom/Dad/caregiver recognizes need and picks up the baby, OR
- Need is met.
- Baby is fed, diaper changed.
- Baby is calm, trust is secure and baby attaches.[9]

DISTURBED ATTACHMENT CYCLE

- Baby has a need; baby cries.
- Need is not recognized.
- No one picks up the baby.
- Baby feels rage: angry, helpless, hopeless.
- Lack of relief; neglected, ignored.
- Baby quits crying because the need is not met. Child becomes passive and withdrawn. No attachment.[10]

DISTURBED ATTACHMENT BEHAVIOR PATTERNS AS AN ADULT:

Along with sexual abuse, child victims may also suffer from neglect, wherein they experience mixed affections from the perpetrator, thus forming a disorganized attachment disorder from the mixed messages they receive.[11]

Ambivalence is when a survivor has mixed feelings or ideas about their perpetrator. For example, they may love the person abusing them because their abuser is a parent or family member. At the same time, they may hate the abuser for what they are doing to them. On one hand, they appreciate the attention or the gifts they have received from their perpetrator; on the other hand, they may hate what it has/will cost them.

EXAMPLES OF DISTURBED ATTACHMENT BEHAVIOR AS AN ADULT:

This can also happen when a child uses their voice and is not believed. If nothing is done, the abuse may continue (Olga's mom dissociated to cope, and the abuse continued; Olga detached and dissociated to cope).

It can also happen when the child is blamed for the abuse.

BIBLICAL EXAMPLE:
(Looking through the eyes of trauma.)

TAMAR'S FILE

Tamar's voice was stolen:
- She pleaded with Amnon, her brother, not to rape her. *He didn't listen.*
- She pleaded again not to throw her out like a piece of garbage or an outcast. *He didn't listen.*
- *She used her voice and told* her brother Absolom, but *he didn't listen.* He told her to keep silent, hush, not to say anything, that it was a *"family matter."*
- David *knew and did nothing*, even though he was king and had the power to administer justice and vindicate his daughter.
- She experienced *rejection—her father chose to protect his son's reputation rather than defend his daughter's safety.*

In 2 Samuel 13:20, Tamar was told not to take this so hard. She lived in her brother Absalom's home, bitter and desolate.

DESOLATE: (of a place) deserted of people and in a state of bleak and dismal emptiness; a state of complete emptiness or destruction; anguished misery or loneliness.

TAMAR'S DETACHMENT:
-
-
-
-
-

SIMILARITIES IN BEHAVIOR

Tamar and Mephibosheth—two survivors of different traumas—both had some things in common:

BEHAVIOR #2: TRUST ISSUES

When the abuse is perpetrated by someone you know, someone you trusted, someone you loved, you tell yourself, "I can't trust anyone." But the truth is, you can't trust everyone.

EXAMPLE OF LIVING BEHIND WALLS

A woman whose husband cheats on her and leaves her for the other woman,

BEHAVIOR #3: IDENTITY CRISIS

WHAT IS AN IDENTITY CRISIS?

An identity crisis is defined as a period of uncertainty and confusion, in which a person's sense of identity becomes insecure, typically due to a change in their expected aims or role in society, and is also a period in which a person loses sight of important aspects of themselves, their personality, preferences, purpose, and/or habits.[12]

Tamar and Mephibosheth both experienced an identity crisis.

BIBLICAL EXAMPLE: MEPHIBOSHETH

> Then the king said, "Is there not still someone of the house of Saul, to whom I may show the kindness of God?" And Ziba said to the king, "There is still a son of Jonathan who is lame in his feet." So the king said to him, "Where is he?" And Ziba said to the king, "Indeed he is in the house of Machir the son of Ammiel, in Lo Debar." Then King David sent and brought him out of the house of Machir the son of Ammiel, from Lo Debar.
>
> Now when Mephibosheth the son of Jonathan, the son of Saul, had come to David, he fell on his face and prostrated himself. Then David said, "Mephibosheth?" And he answered, "Here is your servant!" So David said to him, "Do not fear, for I will surely show you kindness for Jonathan your father's sake, and will restore to you all the land of Saul your grandfather; and you shall eat bread at my table continually." Then he bowed himself, and said, "What is your servant, that you should look upon such a dead dog as I?" (2 Samuel 9:3-8 NLT)

As Mephibosheth grew up, we see that he suffered an identity crisis.

Tamar also suffered an identity crisis:
-
-
-
-

BEHAVIOR #4: TRAUMA IDENTITY

WHAT IS A TRAUMA IDENTITY?

In 2 Samuel 9, Mephibosheth also suffered from a trauma identity.

"For as he thinks in his heart, so is he." (Proverbs 23:7 NKJV)

In his heart, he saw himself as a dead dog. Although he was a prince, all he could see was that he was orphaned. Mephibosheth suffered from a victim mentality.

A trauma identity (victim mentality) causes a person:

-
-
-
-
-
-

Where trauma has happened, there is shame.

Guilt says, "I feel bad for what I did."

Shame says, "I feel bad about who I am."

What they need is to be validated, feel understood, be given a safe place, and be reminded that they are worthy, they are supported, and what they are feeling is normal.

THEY ARE A SURVIVOR

A survivor is someone who doesn't deny the abuse but doesn't allow it to define them or become their identity.

I CAN CHOOSE TO LET IT DEFINE ME, CONFINE ME, REFINE ME, OUTSHINE ME… OR I CAN CHOOSE TO MOVE ON AND LEAVE IT BEHIND ME.

BEHAVIOR #5: FEARS AND PHOBIAS

Trauma causes fear:

-
-
-
-
-

BEHAVIOR #6: BLACK AND WHITE THINKING

ALL ONE WAY OR ALL THE OTHER. IT'S EITHER/OR, NO IN BETWEEN.

If a man was the abuser, the survivor may think that all men are dangerous. If so, we live our lives according to that "fact."

-
-
-
-
-
-
-

BEHAVIOR #7: NEED TO CONTROL

The need to control results when the survivor did not have any control over the abuse, and now the survivor tries to control and plan everything.

THREE PERSONALITY PROFILES OFTEN SEEN IN SURVIVORS

MISS LIFE OF THE PARTY (TRAUMA/STRESS RESPONSE – FLIGHT)

-
-
-
-
-
-
-

MISS INDEPENDENT (TRAUMA/STRESS RESPONSE – FIGHT)

-
-

-
-
-
-
-

MISS CO-DEPENDENT (TRAUMA/STRESS RESPONSE - FREEZE/FAWN)

-
-
-
-
-
-
-
-
-
-
-
-
-
-
-
-

03

Survival Skills

Skills trauma survivors develop in service of survival.

1. SURVIVORS DO WHAT THEY ARE TOLD.

Perpetrators often use fear as a means of control.

THIS SURVIVAL SKILL IN ADULTHOOD

2. SURVIVORS DISSOCIATE.

Most of us experience mild dissociation in our everyday lives.

EXAMPLES OF DISSOCIATION:

SPIRITUAL DISSOCIATION:
Spiritual dissociation is when survivors deny feeling emotions by pretending to be okay based on their religious beliefs such as I don't want to appear weak, I need to be victorious. The truth is Jesus is victorious and it's okay to feel emotions not to deny they exist.

3. SURVIVORS INITIATE THE ABUSE.

A victim knows that the abuse is going to happen but doesn't know when. She will initiate the abuse so that she feels some sense of control. There is a sense of relief.

Often, survivors need to be reminded that the abuse was not their fault. Even if they initiated the anticipated abuse, they did nothing wrong. This was a normal coping mechanism to survive their trauma. They need to be validated. They were brilliant and brave to use their survival skills in order to make it through their abuse.

4. SURVIVORS USE ADAPTIVE COPING STRATEGIES.

TYPES OF ADAPTIVE COPING STRATEGIES:

-
-
-
-
-
-
-
-
-

Helping Survivors Move Forward

Survivors get stuck—stuck in the past, stuck at a particular age that the trauma occurred.

ONE SURVIVOR'S STORY

> I was incapable of taking responsibility for anything that I did wrong. Because of the way I was raised, mistakes are unacceptable. When my sister and I were young, there was no room for error. It didn't matter what the circumstances were, we were expected to perform perfectly. I can remember sitting for hours at the kitchen table of a man my father was drinking with. We were in a ramshackle house with no running water and the man drove a tractor instead of a car. I sat perfectly upright, at the edge of the chair, hands folded neatly in my lap, for five hours. We were never allowed to move or speak without permission, and our instructions were to always decline anything that was offered (i.e. food, drinks, toys, etc). Our stomachs were not supposed to growl, we were not supposed to have to use the restroom, and we were definitely not allowed to ask when we were leaving. Sometimes we stayed in our boots and our winter coats the entire time, as we had to be prepared to leave whenever Dad decided he was ready. I grew up in Canada, so it was typical to be wearing a heavy coat, mittens, a hat and scarf. That makes for a long day sitting motionless beside a woodstove. As an adult, I didn't know that I could ask a question. I didn't know that I could voice a thought or admit that I needed help. For almost thirty-five years I was emotionally stuck in that chair beside the woodstove. I still have difficulty accepting food or drink that is offered to me when I'm at someone's house or business. I tend to be very still or very quiet when I'm under stress. I still don't like asking people if I can use their restroom. Physically, I've been out of that chair for thirty years, but emotionally I sometimes still get stuck there.

WHEN WORKING WITH SOMEONE LIKE THIS BRAVE SURVIVOR:

JESUS' FILE

Even Jesus has scars. How could we relate to Jesus if He didn't have scars? We couldn't. But we can relate to Jesus because we know He understands our pain. How does He understand our pain? He, too, has experienced trauma. If we read the notes in Jesus' file, what would we find?

Jesus knows what it feels like to be abused—physically, emotionally, and sexually exploited. Jesus endured much abuse during His lifetime. Jesus did not die by a method that only lasted seconds or minutes, like being shot or a gas chamber. No. He died a long and excruciating, painful death for us. Let's look at His trauma:

JESUS' FILE

- Jesus was wrongfully accused and imprisoned for a crime He didn't commit.
- While awaiting trial, He was turned over to a mob of angry soldiers.
- He was stripped naked, humiliated in front of everyone, including those He knew.
- He was scorned, treated worse than an animal, rejected as an outcast, and spat on.
- He was mentally abused and bullied, called names, ridiculed, laughed at, made fun of, and tormented.
- The soldiers plucked out His beard.
- He was violently beaten, whipped, and tortured without mercy.
- A crown made from thorns was twisted together and stuck onto His head.
- He was made to wear a purple robe over His open wounds.
- He was sentenced to death.
- Jesus was made to carry a wooden cross—the very instrument they would use to murder Him—up to His place of execution.
- Jesus was nailed to a cross, naked and exposed, exploited in front of all who knew Him, to die an agonizing death.
- He suffered while soldiers gambled for His clothes, laughing and sneering as He hung there to die.
- He endured all this for a crime He didn't commit; He was an innocent victim.

WHAT DO YOU BELIEVE?

LIES VS. TRUTH

LIE: GOD DID THIS TO ME.

ROOT CAUSE:

TRUTH:

> "The thief's purpose is to steal, kill and destroy.
> My purpose is to give life in all its fullness" (John 10:10 TLB).

LIE: IT HAPPENED A LONG TIME AGO, SO IT'S IN THE PAST.

ROOT CAUSE:

TRUTH:

LIE: THE ABUSE WAS MY FAULT.

ROOT CAUSE:

TRUTH:

LIE: I CAN'T TRUST ANYONE.

ROOT CAUSE:

TRUTH:

> "But I trust in your unfailing love.
> I will rejoice because you have rescued me" (Psalm 13:5).

LIE: I CANNOT FEEL.

ROOT CAUSE:

TRUTH:

LIE: EVERYTHING WRONG IN MY LIFE IS "THEIR" FAULT.

ROOT CAUSE:

TRUTH:

LIE: IF I MAKE MYSELF UNATTRACTIVE, I CAN AVOID BEING HURT OR NOTICED.

ROOT CAUSE:

TRUTH:

LIE: SEX IS THE ONLY WAY TO GET MY RELATIONAL NEEDS MET.

ROOT CAUSE:

TRUTH:

LIE: SEX IS BAD.

ROOT CAUSE:

TRUTH:

LIE: MY BODY BETRAYED ME

ROOT CAUSE:

TRUTH:

FORGIVENESS VS. UNFORGIVENESS

> ♡♡
> IF YOU DON'T LET THE PAST DIE,
> THEN IT WON'T LET YOU LIVE.

UNFORGIVENESS TIES US TO THE PAST.

"Watch over each other to make sure that no one misses the revelation of God's grace. And make sure no one lives with a root of bitterness sprouting within them which will only cause trouble and poison the hearts of many" (Hebrews 12:15).

Looking through the eyes of trauma:
Where there is bitterness, there is usually unforgiveness.

TAMAR'S FILE

"Her brother Absalom said to her, 'Has your brother Amnon had his way with you? Now, my dear sister, let's keep it quiet—a family matter. He is, after all, your brother. Don't take this so hard.' Tamar lived in her brother Absalom's home, bitter and desolate."
2 Samuel 13:20 MSG

She was bitter.

WHAT DOES UNFORGIVENESS LOOK LIKE?

Unforgiveness says:

-
-
-
-
-

5 CHARACTERISTICS OF BITTERNESS

1. Justifies bitterness:
2. Overly critical.
3. Secretly celebrates the misfortunes of others.
4. Hurt by one, so all are bad: easily offended.
5. Stuck in the past.

BITTERNESS IS LIKE DRINKING RAT POISON AND WAITING FOR THE RAT TO DIE.

COMMON MYTHS SURVIVORS BELIEVE ABOUT FORGIVENESS

MYTH: IF I FORGIVE, I'M GOING TO GET HURT AGAIN.
   Truth: Forgiveness is not going to hurt you. It's going to free you.

MYTH: IF I FORGIVE, THAT MEANS WHAT WAS DONE TO ME IS ALRIGHT.
   Truth: What was done to you is not okay.

MYTH: TO FORGIVE MEANS TO FORGET.
   Truth: Only God has the power to forgive and forget.

   "Behold, I will bring it health and healing; I will heal them and reveal to them the abundance of peace and truth" (Jeremiah 33:6-7).

WHAT IS FORGIVENESS?
- Forgiveness has to do with punishment.
- Forgiveness is not deserved.
- Forgiveness is a choice.

We need God's help to not only forgive our abuser, but also to help us forgive:
- The person or people who didn't believe us.
- The person or people who were supposed to protect us but didn't.
- Ourselves if we are holding ourselves responsible in any way.

SURVIVOR'S REACH SOME LEVEL OF FORGIVENESS.
Tamar told her brother, and her father knew. Her brother did something.
-
-
- .
-
-

I wonder if Tamar was ever able to forgive them.

Mephibosheth moved forward!
-
-
-
-

I wonder if David shared stories with Mephibosheth about his dear friend Jonathan, Mephibosheth's father.

"I will restore your soul" (Psalm 23).

04

Working With Survivors

CHARACTERISTICS OF AN EFFECTIVE PEER SUPPORTER

There are four essential qualities that enable the counselor to develop a relationship with the client. Although these are expounded upon in secular psychology, they are founded in biblical principles. The more we learn to reflect these qualities, the more effective we will become in helping others and ministering to their needs.

1. EMPATHY

Empathy is the ability to understand what the client is feeling and to communicate that to her, while remaining objective enough to assist her.

To achieve empathy, we must balance the following two qualities:
- Intellectual Consideration:

- Sympathy:

Let's look at the example of the Samaritan:

> Then a despised Samaritan came along, and when he saw the man, he felt com-

passion for him. Going over to him, the Samaritan soothed his wounds with olive oil and wine and bandaged them. Then he put the man on his own donkey and took him to an inn, where he took care of him. The next day he handed the innkeeper two silver coins, telling him, "Take care of this man. If his bill runs higher than this, I'll pay you the next time I'm here." (Luke 10:33-35)

-
-
-

Let's look at Jesus' example: *"But when He saw the multitudes, He was moved with compassion for them because they were weary and scattered, like sheep having no Shepard"* (Matthew 9:36).
Jesus identified with people in need to alleviate their suffering.

> "LIKE ONE WHO TAKES OFF GARMENTS ON A COLD DAY OR LIKE VINEGAR ON SODA, IS HE WHO SINGS TO A TROUBLED HEART."
> PROVERBS 25:20

2. GENUINNESS
Genuineness is being freely oneself.

3. UNCONDITIONAL ACCEPTANCE
Unconditional acceptance means to affirm and care for the person, apart from her lifestyle—not condoning the client's behavior, but accepting her in spite of it.

It's important to examine your heart and ask yourself if you have any prejudices that might restrict you from accepting your client unconditionally, without judgement. Ask yourself if it would disturb you to learn:

WHERE WOULD SHE BE WITHOUT JESUS?

Where would you be without Jesus?

4. HUMILITY

Humility is the ability to recognize your limits as well as your strengths.

JEREMIAH'S EXAMPLE

> So the king told Ebed-melech, "Take thirty of my men with you, and pull Jeremiah out of the cistern before he dies." So Ebed-melech took the men with him and went to a room in the palace beneath the treasury, where he found some old rags and discarded clothing. He carried these to the cistern and lowered them to Jeremiah on a rope. Ebed-melech called down to Jeremiah, "Put these rags under your armpits to protect you from the ropes." Then when Jeremiah was ready, they pulled him out. So Jeremiah was returned to the courtyard of the guard—the palace prison—where he remained. (Jeremiah 38:10-13 NLT)

What we learn from Jeremiah:

> "WHERE THERE IS NO COUNSEL, THE PEOPLE FALL; BUT IN THE MULTITUDE OF COUNSELORS THERE IS SAFETY."
> PROVERBS 11:14

REASONS WE REFER A CLIENT TO ANOTHER PERSON.

1. CONFLICT OF INTEREST

2. A CLIENT THAT IS ACTIVELY SUICIDAL

3. A CLIENT THAT IS UNDER THE INFLUENCE

4. WHEN A LICENSED PROFESSIONAL WORKING WITH THE CLIENT WILL NOT CONSENT TO US WORKING WITH THEM.

5. WHEN YOU FEEL THAT YOU ARE NOT A GOOD FIT FOR THE CLIENT

Sometimes, based on the type of trauma the client is suffering from, it may be in her best interest to refer her to another counselor or professional.

ACTIVATION

In the following statement, listen for and underline the statements that contain ambivalence, a lie, denial, and feelings.

> I don't know what's wrong with me. I always feel like something's wrong with me, like I'm different. It's like I am always on the outside looking in. When I was little, sitting in class, I would hope the teacher wouldn't call on me. I had a difficult time paying attention in class because I couldn't focus. I got bad grades, and my mom would say, "I know you're smarter than this." I was always worried my mom was not going to be there when I got home from school because if she wasn't, then my brother would take advantage of me. I hated being alone with him. I know he didn't mean to hurt me. He told me I better not tell or I would get in trouble. He was my big brother. He took care of me. He even protected me from his guy friends. Why wasn't my mom there? How come she couldn't see what he was doing to me? Anyways, that was a long time ago. I'm fine now.

Now, as a peer supporter, how could you normalize what she has shared?
How could you validate her?
How could you instill hope?

Self-Care

WHAT IS SELF-CARE?

- The practice of taking action to preserve or improve one's own health.
- The practice of taking an active role in protecting one's own well-being and happiness, in particular during periods of stress.

SELF-CARE ASSESSMENT[13]

This assessment tool provides an overview of effective strategies to maintain self-care. After completing the full assessment, choose one item from each area that you will actively work to improve.

Using the scale below, rate the following areas in terms of frequency:

5 = Frequently
4 = Occasionally
3 = Rarely
2 = Never
1 = It never occurred to me

PHYSICAL SELF-CARE

_____ Eat regularly (e.g. breakfast, lunch, and dinner).
_____ Eat healthy.
_____ Exercise.
_____ Get regular medical care for prevention.
_____ Get medical care when needed.
_____ Take time off when needed.
_____ Get messages.
_____ Dance, swim, walk, run, play sports, sing, or do some other fun physical activity.
_____ Make time for intimacy with your partner.
_____ Get enough sleep.
_____ Wear clothes you like.
_____ Take vacations.
_____ Take day trips or mini vacations.

_____ Make time away from telephones.
_____ Other:

PSYCHOLOGICAL SELF-CARE
_____ Make time for self-reflection.
_____ Have your own personal psychotherapy (counseling).
_____ Write in a journal.
_____ Read literature that is unrelated to work.
_____ Do something at which you are not an expert or in charge.
_____ Decrease stress in your life.
_____ Let others know different aspects of you.
_____ Notice your inner experience: listen to your thoughts, judgements, beliefs, attitudes, and feelings.
_____ Engage your intelligence in a new area: go to an art museum, history exhibit, sports event, auction, or theater.
_____ Practice receiving from others.
_____ Be curious.
_____ Say "no" to extra responsibilities sometimes.
_____ Other:

EMOTIONAL SELF-CARE
_____ Spend time with others whose company you enjoy.
_____ Stay in contact with important people in your life.
_____ Give yourself affirmations; praise yourself.
_____ Love yourself.
_____ Re-read favorite books. Re-watch favorite movies.
_____ Identify and seek out comforting activities, objects, people, relationships, and places.
_____ Allow yourself to cry.
_____ Find things that make you laugh.
_____ Express your outrage in social action, letters, and donations, marches, or protests.
_____ Play with children/grandchildren/nieces/nephews.
_____ Other:

SPIRITUAL SELF-CARE
_____ Make time for reflection.
_____ Spend time with nature.
_____ Find a spiritual connection or community.
_____ Be open to inspiration.

_____ Cherish your optimism and hope.
_____ Be aware of nonmaterial aspects of life.
_____ Try at times not to be in charge or the expert.
_____ Be open to not knowing.
_____ Identify what is meaningful to you, and notice its place in your life.
_____ Meditate.
_____ Pray.
_____ Sing.
_____ Spend time with children.
_____ Have experiences of awe relish the moment.
_____ Contribute to causes in which you believe.
_____ Read inspirational literature (talks, music, etc.).
_____ Other:

WORKPLACE OR PROFESSIONAL SELF-CARE

_____ Take a break during the workday (e.g. lunch).
_____ Take time to chat with co-workers.
_____ Make quiet time to complete tasks.
_____ Identify projects or tasks that are exciting and rewarding.
_____ Set limits with your clients or colleagues.
_____ Balance your work load so that no one day or part of a day is "too much."
_____ Arrange your workspace so that it is comfortable and comforting.
_____ Get regular supervision or consultation.
_____ Negotiate for your needs (benefits, pay raise).
_____ Have a peer support group.
_____ Develop a non-trauma area of professional interest.
_____ Other:

BALANCE

_____ Strive for balance within your work life.
_____ Strive for balance among work, family, relationships, play, and rest.

SUGGESTIONS FOR WAYS TO SELF-CARE:

1.
2.
3.
4.

5.
6.
7.
8.
9.
10.
11.
12.
13.
14.
15.
16.
17.
18.
19.
20.
21.
22.
23.
24.
25.
26.
27.
28.

Remember that self-care is not optional; it's essential!

Resources

A DOOR OF HOPE INTERNATIONAL
Kristen Kellett, Founder, CEO
Author of The Cry and SCARS (Survivors Carry A Real Story)

avA- a voice AWAKENING and STRAIGHT OUTTA TRAUMA
Shona Chavis
avoiceAwakening@yahoo.com

Committed to Freedom - Sallie Culbreth
Violated - Book by Mercy Multiplied
The Sum of My Parts - Book by Olga Trujillo
Tootles the Turtle Tells the Truth - Book by Lenell Levy Melancon

OTHER SCARS TRAUMA TRAININGS INCLUDE:

- Trauma
- Domestic Violence
- Addiction
- Abortion
- Grief
- Suicide Intervention
- SCARS Workbook: Survivor's Guide to Trauma Recovery

NATIONAL HOTLINES

ABORTION	(888) 510-BABY
ADDICTION	(800) 662-HELP
CHILD ABUSE	(800) 4-A-CHILD
DOMESTIC VIOLENCE	(800) 799-7233
GRIEF	(800) 445-4808

HUMAN TRAFFICKING	(800) 373-7888
SEXUAL ASSAULT	(800) 656-HOPE
SUICIDE	(800) 273-8255 or 988

Thank you for all you do to help trauma survivors.

YOUR VOICE. YOUR STORY. IT MATTERS.

Exit Survey

(PLEASE COMPLETE AND RETURN BEFORE LEAVING)

1. On a scale of 1-10, with 10 = highly informative and 1 = somewhat informative, what would you rate this training? _____

2. Would you recommend this training to others? Y N

3. Would you like to be contacted when future trainings become available? Y N

4. Which other training(s) are you interested in?
   - Grief
   - Trauma
   - Domestic Violence
   - Abortion
   - Addiction
   - Suicide Intervention

5. Would you consider hosting a training in your area? Y N

6. Are you interested in training others? Y N

7. What will you take away from this training? (What stood out to you the most? What did you learn?)

8. What was your least favorite part of the training?

9. Anything else you would like us to know?

10. Would you be interested in attending SCARS Retreat (for survivors)? Y N

Name: _____
Email: _____
Phone: _____
Address: _____

ENDNOTES

1. Warning signs. RAINN. (n.d.). https://www.rainn.org/warning-signs
2. Davis, S. (2021, April 5). Childhood sexual abuse and complex post-traumatic stress disorder. CPTSD Foundation. https://cptsdfoundation.org/2021/04/05/childhood-sexual-abuse-and-complex-post-traumatic-stress-disorder/
3. Info & Stats for Journalists. National Sexual Violence Resource Center. (2015). https://www.nsvrc.org/sites/default/files/publications_nsvrc_factsheet_media-packet_statistics-about-sexual-violence_0.pdf
4. Parish, Bobbi L. "Part Two: Creating a Trigger Tool Kit." Certified Trauma Specialist Program [Online Course]. International Association of Trauma Recovery Coaching. 2022. https://certifiedtraumarecoverycoaching.com/certified-trauma-specialist-program
5. Brown, C. (2020). Free Cyntoia: My search for redemption in the American prison system. Atria Books.
6. Warning signs. RAINN. (n.d.). https://www.rainn.org/warning-signs
7. Mayo Foundation for Medical Education and Research. (2022, December 13). Post-traumatic stress disorder (PTSD). Mayo Clinic. https://www.mayoclinic.org/diseases-conditions/post-traumatic-stress-disorder/symptoms-causes/syc-20355967
8. Mayo Foundation for Medical Education and Research. (2022, December 13). Post-traumatic stress disorder (PTSD). Mayo Clinic. https://www.mayoclinic.org/diseases-conditions/post-traumatic-stress-disorder/symptoms-causes/syc-20355967
9. Hasson, A. (2011, April 27). What's the Connection? Adoption & Attachment. Upside Down Therapy. http://upsidedowntherapy.blogspot.com/2011/04/whats-connection-adoption-attachment.html
10. W, J. (2011, April 28). Control Continued. Rearing, RAD & Recipes. http://rearingradrecipes.blogspot.com/2011/04/control-continued.html
11. Davis, S. (2021, April 5). Childhood sexual abuse and complex post-traumatic stress disorder. CPTSD Foundation. https://cptsdfoundation.org/2021/04/05/childhood-sexual-abuse-and-complex-post-traumatic-stress-disorder/
12. Identity crisis: Causes, symptoms, and ways to cope. BetterUp. (n.d.). https://www.betterup.com/blog/identity-crisis#:~:text=An%20identity%20crisis%20is%20defined,can%20happen%20at%20any%20time.
13. Saakvitne, K. W., & Pearlman, L. A. (1996). Transforming the pain: A workbook on vicarious traumatization. W.W. Norton & Company.

www.ingramcontent.com/pod-product-compliance
Lightning Source LLC
Chambersburg PA
CBHW080416170426
43194CB00015B/2828